ARMOURS OF I

Henry VIII, like his royal contemporaries, lived sumptuously and was attended by wealthy courtiers. But these facts alone do not explain why many of the finest armours and the more interesting arms now in the Tower date from his reign in particular, why they were mostly his own property, for use by either himself or his bodyguard, or why the Armouries today still convey an impression of his personality and authority.

At a time when magnificence signified power, Henry's desire for prestige inevitably led him into displays of costly splendour. By nature he was an active sportsman, and until obesity overcame him he had an innate ability to excel in martial skills. Such circumstances and gifts inspired in him a deep interest in the use and technical development of armour and weapons, an interest which, for very similar reasons, was shared by his royal contemporaries, the Emperors Maximilian I and his grandson Charles V, and Francis I, King of France.

The Emperors of the Holy Roman Empire had the greatest armourers in Europe at their command for the supply of magnificent garnitures of armour and costly arms. Henry had no such facilities. He could only secure the services of lesser craftsmen, not in imperial employ, and the situation in England is indicated by the fact that for a century or more before Henry succeeded to the throne those Englishmen who could afford fine armour and arms ordered them from Flanders, South Germany or north Italy. Thus Henry VIII, obviously dissatisfied with the national inferiority, in about 1511 persuaded

a number of Italian armourers to come to England and these he established in workshops by his palace at Greenwich. This was at about the time the Emperor Maximilian presented him with a splendid armour, of which the grotesque helmet in the Armouries (page 8) is probably the only surviving part. The inability to reciprocate with a like gift may well have spurred him on to establish his own Court workshops.

The Tower Armouries now contain four of Henry's personal armours, a fifth survives at Windsor, and modern scholars have suggested that a further two now in the Metropolitan Museum, New York, belonged to him. The earlier two, the tonlet or skirted armour (page 6), and the engraved and silver-gilt armour (page 10), both in the Tower, pose problems of origin. They display definite Italian characteristics yet they also have features of a distinctive kind which may have originated and been developed in the Court workshops of Burgundy and spread thence throughout much of north-western Europe. The tonlet armour for use in foot combat dates from about 1512 when Henry was a handsome slim young man 6ft 2ins tall. The engraved and silver-gilt armour of about 1515, which displays the linked initials H and K for Henry himself and his wife Katherine of Aragon, could have been the work of two Italians, Filippo de Grampis and Giovanni Angelo de Littis; but it could equally well have been made by Flemish armourers for the reason stated, namely, that it has features not generally found in Italian productions. Technically it is a field armour, but such was its original splendour, engraved may also have been the work of an unknown Flemish armourer in the employ of the Hapsburgs. The style of the engraved decoration again suggests the hand of Paul van Vrelant.

In about 1515 Henry established in lodgings and workshops in his palace at Greenwich a team of German and Flemish armourers under a Master Armourer, Martin van Royne. This establishment, which created a characteristic style of its own, survived until the outbreak of the Civil War in 1642. Henry's own foot-combat armour in the Tower (page 16) may well be one of the earliest productions of these craftsmen at Greenwich, for in certain features it seems to anticipate some of the particular characteristics later developed there. In its technical details it is a remarkable example of craft virtuosity. It indicates a slight increase in the girth of the King's torso and limbs as compared with the toilet and silver-gilt armours, thus suggesting that a date of about 1520 should perhaps be assigned to it.

With one exception, all the later surviving armours believed to have been Henry's personal equipment were made at Greenwich. These include two dated garnitures, one of 1527, one of 1540, and a third of about 1545. The first of these, now in the Metropolitan Museum, New York, is known as the 'Genouilhac' armour; the other two are described below. Still in the Tower are also fragments of two, possibly three, other armour garnitures almost certainly made at Greenwich for the King. Firstly, the inventory of his personal armoury made after his death in 1547 has an entry for a 'complete harness' with a crinet (horse's neck-defence) 'with scales parcel graven and gilt' which well describes the decoration of a crinet in the Armouries (page 19). Secondly, a falling buffe (chin and face defence) for attachment to a close helmet, a toepiece for a mail shoe and a pair of saddle steels with etched and gilt borders and delicate scroll decoration (page 18) are i[n] size, quality and form similar to some of the other Henrician pieces. Thirdly, of comparable quality is

and silver-gilt, that it must surely have been made for parade use. The base (skirt), as opposed to the practical skirt of the toilet armour, is an affectation in imitation of the civilian fabric garment of the period and may well have been inspired by a similar feature on Maximilian's gift armour.

The horse armour (page 10) matching the engraved and silver-gilt armour is known to have been engraved by Paul van Vrelant between 1514 and 1519, and such is the similarity of the engraving on the two they must both have been decorated at about the same time. Paul had a workshop in Brussels; he also held a royal appointment to Henry VIII, and the presumption is that he had a workshop in England too. The horse armour is almost certainly Flemish since there are nearly identical horse armours in the armoury of Charles V still at Madrid, as well as comparable pieces decorated by Paul.

Also in the Tower Armouries and of the early years of Henry's reign are a breast and backplate from a tilt armour stamped with a crowned w which is probably the mark of a Flemish armourer. These are of the size of the breast and back of the engraved and silver-gilt armour and similar to others made in Flanders for the Emperor Maximilian and now in the armoury in Vienna.

Two contemporary horse armours in the Tower are also of importance: one (page 14) is possibly the work of Italian craftsmen at Greenwich; the other (page 12), called the 'Burgundian Bard', is unique. Originally silvered and probably gilt, the latter is engraved and embossed with the pomegranate badge of the House of Aragon, the *cross raguly* and the fire-steels emblem of the Order of the Golden Fleece. It could thus have been another gift from Maximilian to Henry as a Knight of the Order, which he became in 1506, or it could have had to do with the occasion of Henry's marriage with Katherine of Aragon in 1509. The 'Burgundian Bard' bears the same maker's mark as that on the engraved and silver-gilt horse armour and therefore

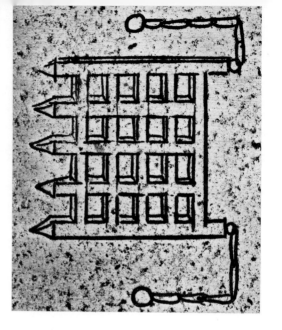

Detail of decoration on horse armour of about 1515 (page 14)

Detail of the decoration on the skirt of Henry's foot-combat armour of about 1512 (page 6).

a single shaffron (horse's head-defence) of about 1530 with alternate bright and gilt bands entirely etched with Classical ornament (page 19) which could well have been part of a complete horse armour or an armour garniture made for his use.

Henry continued to have armour made for his own person almost to the end of his life, for much of the large garniture of his dated 1540 remains in the Tower (page 20). Many pieces are missing, but enough survives to make a brave showing, and the showing is indubitably of Henry VIII. Despite the further thickening of the King's body and legs, the existence of the armour proves that at 49 years of age he was still capable of taking part in jousts, tournaments and foot combats, and even in war (see the diagrams on the front and back covers showing the different ways in which this garniture could be assembled for these purposes). The decorative etched and gilt borders of the plates are in part possibly based upon designs by Hans Holbein, Henry's court painter.

Henry's rapidly increasing obesity is however shown most dramatically by the armour of his made at Greenwich in about 1545 (page 23) which was in the Tower until 1916 when transferred to Windsor Castle, where it now is. It is still larger in girth than the 1540 armour; even so, the thigh and knee defences have had to be cut away to allow the King's swollen legs to rest more comfortably in the saddle. Perhaps more than any other of his armours it reveals with striking immediacy the great stature and bulk of the man.

This completes the account of Henry's armour easily to be seen in this country. Something should however be said of the Master Craftsmen who doubtless made, or supervised the making of, his impressive later armours. By about 1540 Martin van Royne, the Master of the royal workshops at Greenwich, was old, and he was succeeded by the Chief Armourer Erasmus Kyrkenar, presumably a German in origin. Both the 1540 and c.1545 armours where Henry met Francis I, £500 paid for swords of various kinds alone; this was excluding the cost of armour and of setting up an armoury and workshop for the occasion at Guisnes. The clothing and horse bards for the King and courtiers cost over £3,000. Thus the fragmentary remains of Henry VIII's personal armoury today suggest little of the original splendour of his armours and accoutrements. The rich and elaborate saddles, horse-trappings and other equipment long housed in the royal palaces of Westminster and Greenwich and listed in some detail in the 1547 inventory no longer exist. In this the nation is less fortunate than the Austrians and the Spaniards who retain so many of the perishable possessions of the Hapsburgs still to be seen and admired at Vienna, Ambras and Madrid.

Nevertheless, with the help of documents and the few surviving Tudor royal possessions it is possible to visualise something of the colour and pageantry surrounding Henry and, indeed, to picture Henry himself from the Spring of youth to the Autumn of middle age. Today his and his courtiers' armours, overcleaned, robbed and neglected by their custodians as they have been over the past three hundred years, are still impressive examples of the armourers' craft. They are a credit not only to the men who made them but also to the King who wanted, and had, the best for himself and his entourage.

H. R. ROBINSON

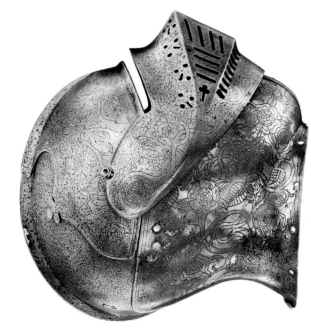

Close-helmet of Henry's engraved and silvered armour of about 1515 (page 10).

exhibit the same high standard of craftsmanship and considered ingenuity with which the iron plates are fashioned to allow maximum freedom of movement to a man not only large and fat but also badly crippled by disease. Contrary to popular belief neither Henry VIII nor any other man clad in complete armour needed a crane to hoist him into the saddle. The only aid needed by a man of the King's great size was a mounting-block, and it is on record that late in life Henry had an extra step added to one he used!

It may be interesting to indicate, by comparison of expenditure, the opulent magnificence of Henry's tournaments. In 1515 the great 900-ton warship *Great Elizabeth* was bought for £2,300. In 1511 the tournament and masques at Westminster cost £4,400. At the 'Field of Cloth of Gold' in 1520,

opposite: Henry VIII on a barded (apparelled) horse. Line and watercolour drawing possibly from a series of designs for the 'Field of Cloth of Gold' (1520). BM ms. Augustus IIIa. *By Courtesy of the Trustees of the British Library*

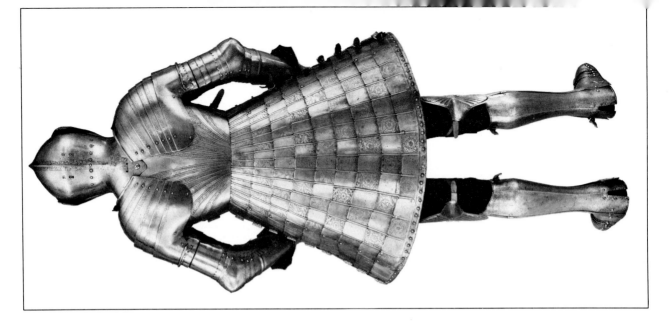

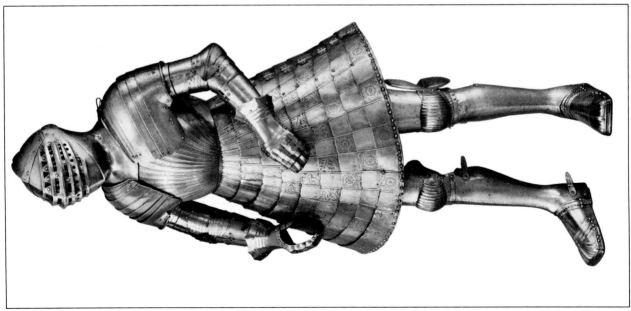

Foot-combat armour, about 1512

Henry VIII's tonlet or skirted armour for foot-combat dating from about 1512 when he was twenty-one years old. Excepting the Milanese helmet, it was probably made by Flemings working in England. The etched decoration has a sketchiness common to much Italian and Flemish etching of the period; it includes the Collar and lesser George of the Order of the Garter around the neck and the Garter below the left knee, Tudor roses on the lower plates of the skirt and the Virgin and Child and St. George on the helmet and on the shoulders.

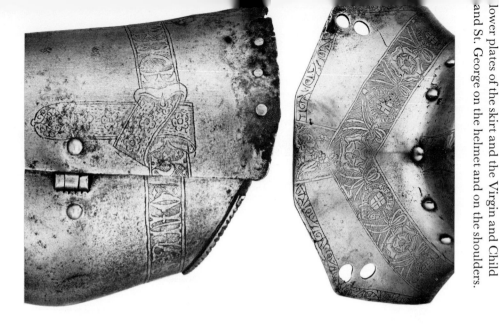

7

Ram's horn helmet, 1514

Probably the sole survivor of an armour presented to Henry VIII by the Emperor Maximilian I in 1514 and made by the Imperial Court Armourer Conrad Seusenhofer of Innsbruck. The pierced and embossed silver-gilt *appliqués* formerly in the sunk panels are now all gone. In the 19th century it was associated with other miscellaneous pieces and exhibited as the armour of Will Summers, Henry VIII's jester! Despite alterations and mutilations it remains a remarkable example of the armourer's craft.

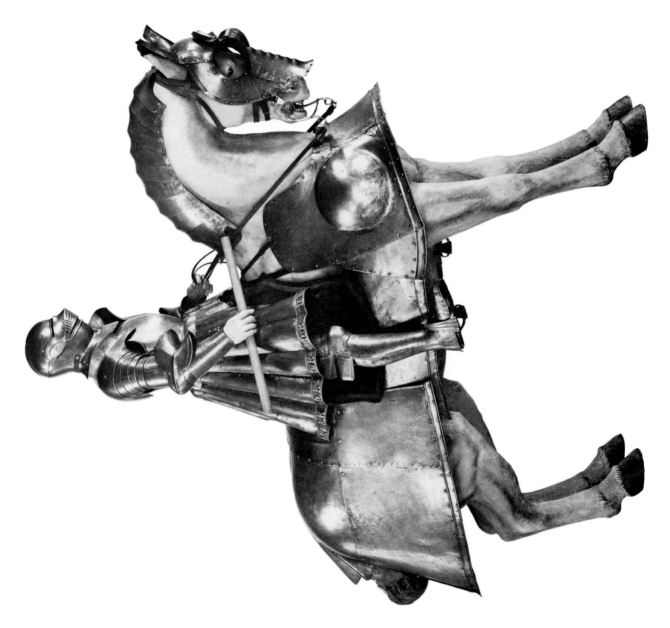

Engraved and silvered armour, about 1515

Armour for man and horse made presumably between 1514 and 1519; for the man perhaps at Greenwich by Filippo de Grampis and Giovanni Angelo de Littis, who were Italians; for the horse perhaps in Flanders and known to have been decorated by Paul van Vrelant of Brussels between the dates stated. Technical features suggest that the man's armour was for use both in the field and in the tournament. The decoration throughout consists of an overall pattern of entwined foliage with roses, pomegranates and other badges of the Houses of

Tudor and Aragon; encircling, on the breast and backplates, the figures of St. George and St. Barbara and, on the horse armour, scenes from the lives of these saints. The initials of Henry VIII and Katherine of Aragon, his first wife, in gilt-bronze decorate the skirt of the engraved and silver-gilt armour. The letters are linked in pairs by true lovers' knots.

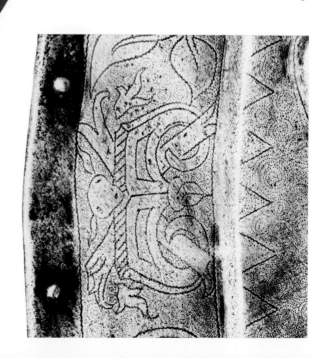

'Burgundian Bard' (horse armour), about 1515
The surface is embossed and engraved and was formerly silver-gilt. (The neck-defence, though contemporary and possibly made for the King's use, does not belong.) Detail shows engraved and punched decoration.

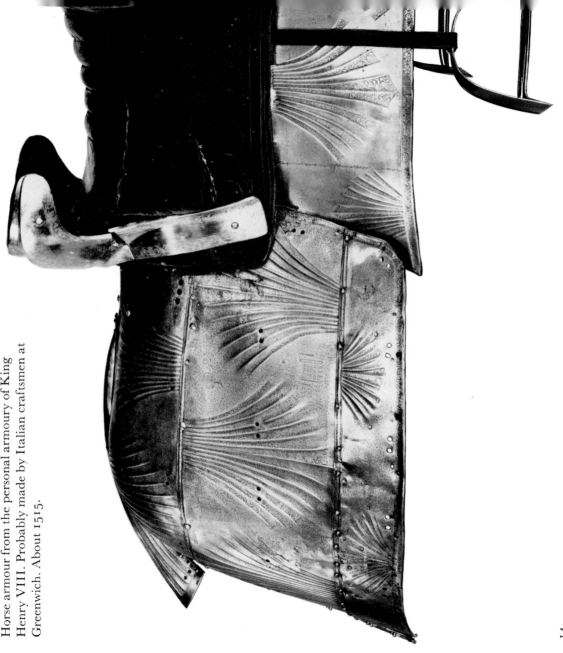

Shaffron 1540 (right)
Defence for horse's head, belonging to Henry VIII's 1540 armour garniture.

Greenwich armour (below)
Horse armour from the personal armoury of King Henry VIII. Probably made by Italian craftsmen at Greenwich. About 1515.

14

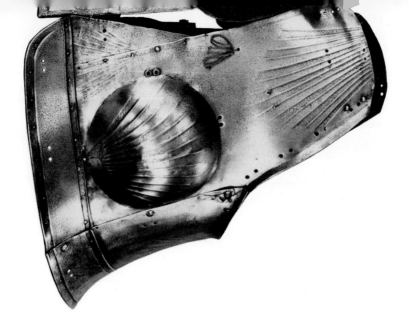

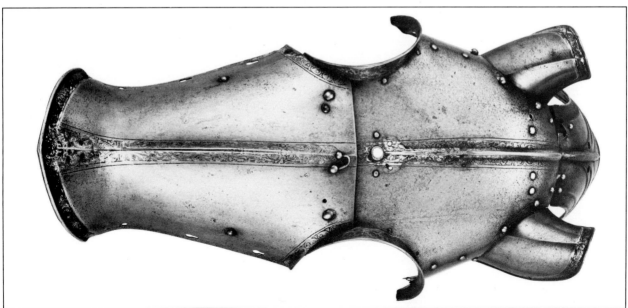

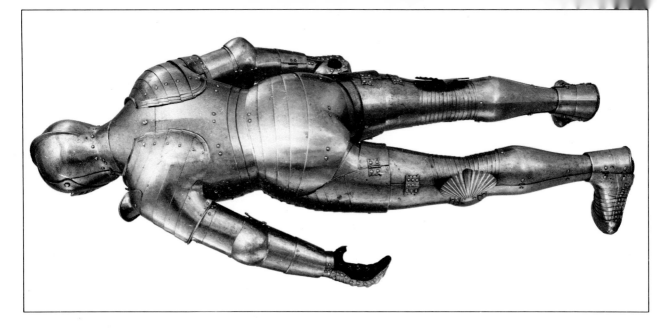

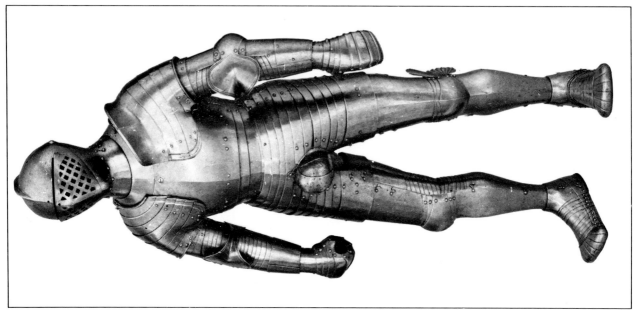

Foot-combat armour, about 1520

Probably made in about 1520 by his Almain armourers newly established at Greenwich under the Master Martin van Royne. This intricate piece of mechanism was left rough from the hammer, and may indeed never have been completely finished. The plates protecting every part of the body weigh a total of 94lbs (42.68kg) and fix the King's height at 6ft 2ins (1.88m) since they are so interrelated that the armour could not be worn by a shorter or taller man. The right gauntlet locks so that a weapon could not be wrested or struck from the hand. (The upstanding neck-guard is missing from the right side, so too is the reinforcing plate from over the brow. The latter was a necessary extra defence against blows to the head from a pollaxe, a favourite weapon in foot combat.)

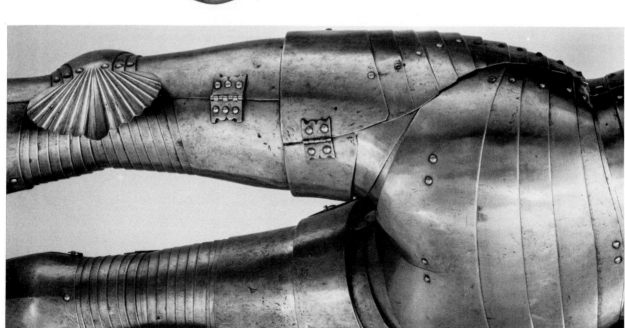

Remains of a lost armour, about 1530

Falling buffe, bevor and gorget plates (protection for the face and neck) which, with a toe cap and a pair of saddle steels, alone survive from a lost armour of Henry VIII. A date in the 1530's is suggested by the evident thickness of the King's neck. Though the etched and gilt decoration are Italianate, the form and character of the plates are typical of Greenwich workmanship.

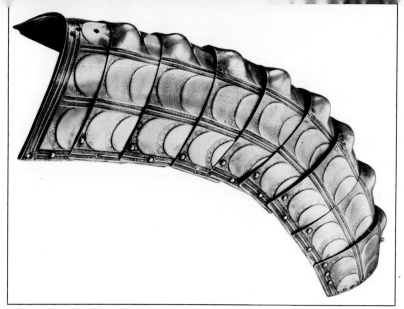

Shaffron, about 1530 (right)
(Defence for horse's head) richly decorated. Though similar in form and construction to the shaffron with Henry VIII's armour garniture made at Greenwich in 1540, the double borders and overall decoration suggest an earlier date, about 1530. (The detachable side plates are lost.)

Crinet 1530 (below)
(Defence for horse's neck), Greenwich work of about 1530. The form and double borders of the plates closely resemble those of the Greenwich armour dated 1527 now in the Metropolitan Museum, New York, which may well have belonged to Henry VIII.

Greenwich armour, 1540

The date is etched on the collar. The decoration is confined to etched and gilded borders; the rest is burnished bright. The armour is part of a large set of pieces, known as a garniture, which could be put together in different ways for different purposes, for war and for the tournament (see diagrams inside front and back covers). As here shown it would have been used for foot combat, though various pieces are now lost. Obviously the prominent cod-piece could not have been worn on horse-back. A most unusual feature of this garniture is the corset (ventral plate) which was strapped right to the body and to which the superimposed plates were bolted. Thus the latter was 'sprung' on an internal harness so that their dead weight was taken off the shoulders and distributed. The only other similar corset known is part of the 1527 Greenwich armour in New York, which may too have belonged to Henry VIII. Detail (below) is of the etched decoration and the date on the collar.

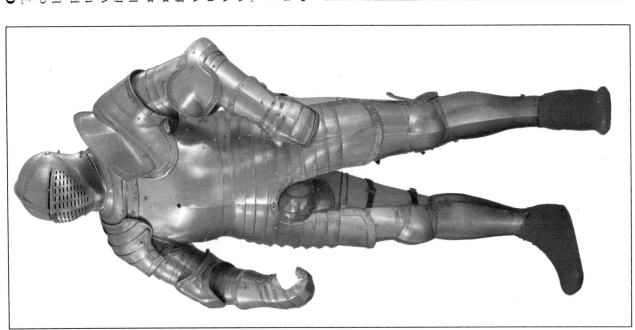

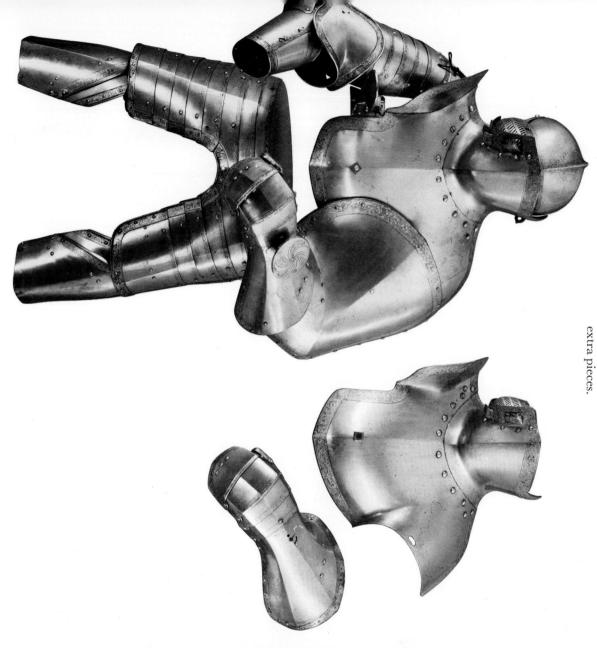

Extra pieces for the Greenwich armour, 1540
(left) The separate pieces of the garniture for attachment for purposes of the tilt. (right) Further extra pieces.

Locking-gauntlet 1540

One of two, belonging to Henry VIII's 1540 armour garniture. Used in the tournament, the finger-plate was locked to the wrist-plate so to prevent a weapon being wrested or knocked from the hand.

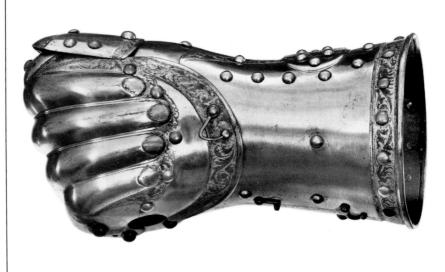

Corset 1540

The corset (ventral plate) formerly connected by shoulder and side straps to a similar backplate (missing). Worn under the cuirass (breast and back plates), the breast-plate of which was bolted to it.

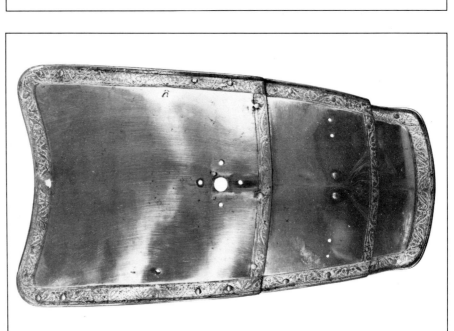

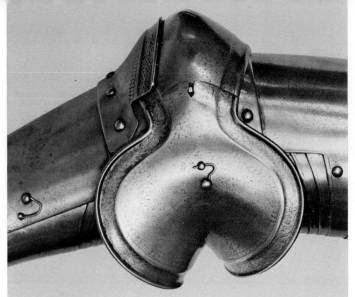

Greenwich armour, about 1545

Formerly in the Tower but now kept at Windsor Castle. It may have been part of an armour garniture like the 1540 garniture, but very much less survives (the visor belongs to the Tower's armour; and the right gauntlet is from a late 16th-century Greenwich armour also in the Tower). The cuirass displays remarkable ingenuity in construction, for the laminations at the waist and upper thighs are so skilfully leathered and slotted for rivets that they could adapt exactly to the movement of a fat man. The gilt borders originally had etched decoration of strapwork and pellets but after years of over-cleaning few traces of gilding remain and the etching is almost obliterated. This armour is possibly the last one made for the King by the Greenwich Master Erasmus Kyrkenar who succeeded old Martin van Royne in about 1540. (See also overleaf.)

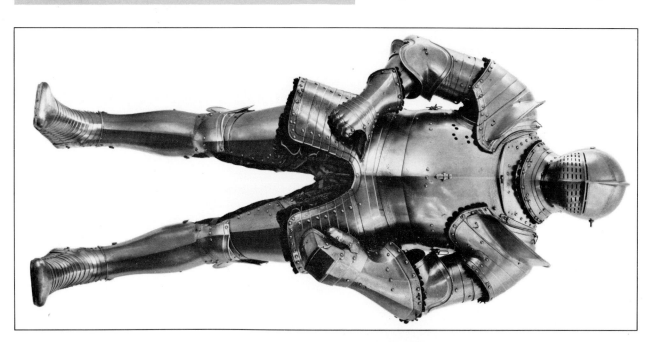

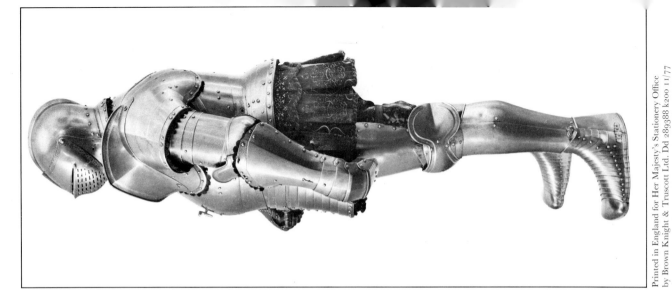

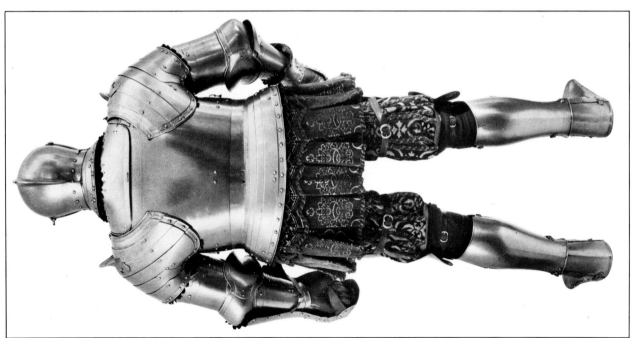

Printed in England for Her Majesty's Stationery Office
by Brown Knight & Truscott Ltd. Dd 289388 k200 11/77